D1462238

Recipes from Provence and Nice

Dominique Compans

Translated by Angela Caldwell

RECIPES FROM PROVENCE AND NICE

Unless otherwise indicated, the photographs of dishes are by the author; landscapes are by Editions Gisserot.

ÉDITIONS JEAN-PAUL GISSEROT
www.editions-gisserot.com

INTRODUCTION

Traditional recipes from Provence, with olive oil as their basic ingredient, are a perfect match for the fresh produce that grows so abundantly in this fertile region and local herbs (rosemary, thyme, bay and sage) bring out the full flavour of the delicious local vegetables.

Garlic, with its powerful and sometimes mysterious taste, is used with onions to add yet more flavour to a "tian", making it more than just another "gratin".

And what could be more natural and mouthwatering than a good ratatouille? Its colours alone stir vivid memories of holidays in Provence!

With its accent mainly on vegetables and fish (bouillabaisse, bourride) and the occasional use of starch (chickpea meal), Provençal cookery and its variations from Nice are highly digestible, whatever some people think, on condition that the ingredients are all top-quality.

PISSALADIÈRE (Nice)

Serves 6
Preparation time: 25 mins.
Baking time: 30 mins.

- *250g flaky pastry*
- *600g thinly-sliced onions*
- *A good number of local olives (decoration)*
- *5 salted anchovies (optional)*
- *Salt, pepper*
- *2 dsp. olive oil*
- *Herbes de Provence (thyme, rosemary) and 3 bay leaves*

Heat the olive oil in a high-sided frying pan and added the thinly-chopped onions. Sprinkle with herbs, salt and pepper. Cover the pan and gently fry the onions for 15 mins. until transparent, taking care not to let them colour. Remove from heat as soon as they are slightly golden. Remove the bay leaves and set aside. Roll out the flaky pastry. Oil a 25cm round cake tin and line with the pastry. Prick the base with a fork to prevent the pastry from bubbling

photo Dufresse

up. Set the oven to Thermostat 6 (medium oven). Cover the pastry with the cooked onions and decorate the top with olives from Nice. Add some more pepper, being careful not to use too much. Bake the Pissaladière for 30 mins. This has even more flavour if you leave it to cool before serving.

A Pissaladière can also be more traditionally made with bread dough. See the pizza recipe.

TAPENADE (Marseille)

Serves 4
Preparation time: 25 mins.
No cooking.

- *250g black olives*
- *100g salted anchovies*
- *100g capers*
- *4 dsp. olive oil*
- *1 clove garlic*
- *Thyme*
- *Pepper*

Remove the stones from the olives. To prepare the anchovies, remove the bones under running water (and the heads if this has not already been done)then rinse well in fresh water to remove all

the salt. Rinse the capers. Crush the ingredients and the garlic with a pestle and mortar for a few minutes until they are all well blended. Strain through a sieve and add to 4 dsp. olive oil, mixing well to form a smooth paste. Add a generous amount of pepper. This paste is spread on small slices of bread and served with an aperitif. It stores very well in an airtight jar for several days.

ANCHOÏADE (Provence)

Serves 4
Preparation time: 20 mins.
Cooking time: 5 mins.

- *4 cloves garlic*
- *400g salted anchovies*
- *8 dsp. olive oil*
- *½ lemon (juice only)*
- *8 slices bread*
- *Pepper*

Press the garlic in a cloth and set aside the juice that is extracted. Remove the salt from the anchovies under running water and remove the head and central bone. Place the anchovy fillets in an earthenware casserole and add a few spoonfuls of oil and the garlic juice. Blend with a wooden spoon over a very low heat, gradually adding the remainder of the oil to form a smooth past. Add pepper, the juice of half a lemon and spread on toasted bread. The same seasoning can be used for pasta, adding a few spoonfuls of olive oil. Anchoïade keeps easily for several weeks in a glass jar, covered with oil.

SALADE NIÇOISE (Nice)

Serves 4
Preparation time: 15 mins.

- *4 tomatoes (ripe but still firm)*
- *1 medium onion*
- *4 hard-boiled eggs*
- *100g local olives (from Nice)*
- *100g baby broad beans (in season)*
- *1 small green pepper (capsicum)*
- *6 large radish (sliced)*
- *Olive oil*
- *No vinegar*
- *1 clove garlic*
- *1 dozen salted anchovies*

photo Dufresse

Rub a salad bowl with the clove of garlic. Remove any excess garlic and add the following ingredients, in the order given. Cut the tomatoes into medium-sized quarters and thinly slice the pepper. Thinly slice the onion and slice the radish into disks. Wash the anchovies to remove the salt and remove the central bone and head (this gives you anchovy fillets). Add the olives and broad beans, then lay the halved boiled eggs and anchovies decoratively on top. Season moderately with salt and pepper because the anchovies remain slightly salty. Pour over some olive oil.

AUBERGINE LOAF (Nice)

Serves 6
Preparation time: 40 mins.
Cooking time: 25 mins.

- *1 kg aubergines (eggplants)*
- *3 red peppers (capsicum)*
- *2 onions*
- *2 cloves garlic*
- *3 eggs*
- *5 biscottes (toast)*
- *2 pinches herbes de Provence*
- *Tomato sauce*

photo Dufresse

Steam the vegetables separately in a pan without peeling them. Strain the vegetables through a vegetable ricer, using a fairly large grill. Add the eggs (beaten) and biscottes (crushed) then season with salt and pepper and sprinkle with 2 pinches herbes de Provence. Pour the mixture into a medium-sized loaf tin and bake in a moderate oven (Thermostat 6) for 20 mins. As soon as the loaf is cooked, remove it from the oven and carefully tip it out of the tin onto a serving dish. Pour tomato sauce round it. This starter can be eaten hot or cold.

BAGNA CAUDA (Nice)

Serves 4
Preparation time: 10 mins.
Cooking time: 10 mins.

- *200g butter*
- *100g oil*
- *1 cup tomato puree*
- *6 anchovies*
- *2 truffles*
- *4 cloves garlic*
- *Salt, pepper*

Place the butter and oil in a pan. Rinse the anchovies to remove the salt, crush them well with a pestle and mortar and add them to the pan. Cook for 10 mins. Then add the garlic and tomato puree. Season with salt and pepper. Remove from the heat and beat the sauce as if you were making.

PAN BAGNA (Nice)

Serves 4
Preparation time: 20 minutes

4 round country rolls
Olive oil (small glass)
50g Nice olives
2 hard-boiled eggs
1 small green pepper (capsicum)
2 firm tomatoes (not too ripe)
16 anchovy fillets (with salt removed)
A few slices of radish
A small onion cut into rings

Slice open the rolls horizontally. Remove some of the dough from the middle of the two halves. Dampen the interior of the rolls with plenty of olive oil. On the base of the rolls (the flat half) place slices of tomato, a few onion rings, a few slices of radish and a few slices of hard-boiled egg. Add the black Nice olives and the green pepper (sliced). To finish, lay 4 anchovy fillets on the top to form a cross. Do not add too much salt (the anchovies are slightly salty) but season with pepper. If liked, add a few drops of vinegar. Cover with the upper half of the roll. Do the same for each roll. If you want to take the Pan Bagna on a picnic, wrap them individually in greaseproof paper or aluminium foil.

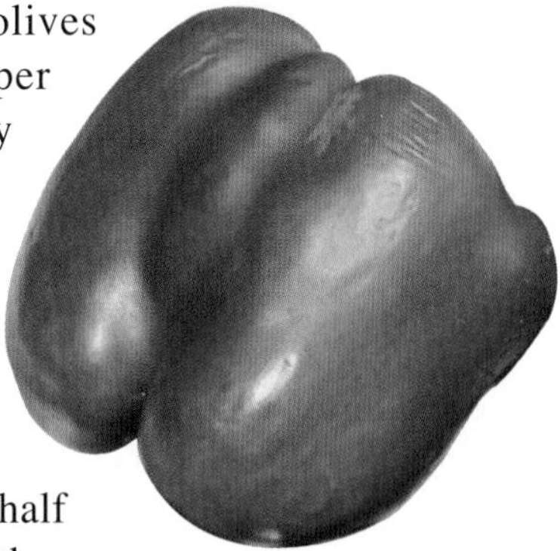

SALADE D'ORANGES AUX OLIVES (Biot)

Serves 4
Preparation time: 15 mins.
No cooking

4 to 6 very sweet oranges
1 handful black Nice olives
Salt, pepper
Olive oil
1 handful baby spinach

Lay a bed of raw baby spinach on a plate. Place the finely sliced orange on top then season with salt and pepper. Pour on some olive oil and add the black olives. Leave to marinate for approximately 1 hour. Serve with toast.

This recipe was given to me by Magali Ghiglione from Biot.

CRESPEOU "Omelette Cake" (Biot)

Serves 6
Preparation time: 1 hr.
Cooking time: 35 mins. for the various omelettes

8 large eggs or 12 small eggs (2 to 3 eggs per omelette)
1 tin tomato sauce (very small size)
Basil leaves (chopped)
1 clove garlic (crushed)
Salt, pepper
4 onions (chopped)
1 pinch thyme
4 dsp. ground nut or sunflower oil
6 artichoke hearts and bases
1 small bunch chard leaves (boiled)

Make 4 light, dry omelettes as indicated below. (recipes overleaf)

TOMATO OMELETTE

Place 1 dsp. oil in a frying pan and heat. Beat 2 or 3 eggs, adding the chopped basil (a few leaves only), tomato sauce, finely crushed garlic, salt and pepper. Pour into the pan and make a light, dry omelette. Set aside on a plate.

CHARD OMELETTE

Cook the leaves of a bunch of chard in a pan of boiling water. Drain well. Beat 2 or 3 eggs and add the cooked chard. Season with salt and pepper. Make an omelette, placing 1 dsp. oil in a hot pan. Ensure that the omelette is light.

ONION OMELETTE

Place 1 dsp. oil in a pan and gently fry the chopped onions with a pinch of thyme, salt and pepper. Set aside. Beat 2 or 3 eggs depending on their size and add the onions. Make an omelette in a hot, oiled pan, as described above. Set aside.

ARTICHOKE OMELETTE

Gently fry 6 little artichoke hearts and bases, with salt and pepper then add 2 or 3 beaten eggs and make a dry omelette. Set aside.

Using a platter that can be put in the fridge, lay out a few basil leaves for decoration (or parsley if you prefer) and layer the omelettes on top, beginning with the tomato omelette, followed by the chard omelette, the onion omelette and, finally, the artichoke omelette. Leave in the refrigerator for approximately 1 hour. When ready to serve, turn the Crepeou over onto a plate and cut it like a cake. This is a summer dish that can be served with a mesclun (mixed leaf) salad seasoned with olive oil and dotted with pine nuts.

ed. Gisserot

POUTINE OMELETTE (Cros-de-Cagnes, Nice)

Serves 2
Preparation time : 10 mins.
Cooking time : 6 mins.

- *100g poutine (small Mediterranean fish)*
- *4 eggs*
- *Salt, pepper*
- *½ clove garlic*
- *Parsley (chopped)*
- *1 dsp. sunflower or ground nut oil*

Quickly rinse the poutine under fresh running water above a very fine-meshed sieve. Beat the eggs in a bowl ready to make an omelette. Season with salt and pepper, add the chopped garlic and parsley then add the rinsed fish. Heat 1 dsp. oil in a frying pan and, when hot, pour in the above mixture and cook for no more than 3 mins. The omelette should be "soft". Serve immediately.

Poutine, sold off carts by fishermen's wives in the streets of Old Nice, is the name given to young fish caught on the shores of the Mediterranean early in the morning, at Le Cros-de-Cagnes. Fishing takes place in February and March but lasts for no more than three weeks. Connoisseurs consider poutine to be at its best when the flesh is fine and translucent.

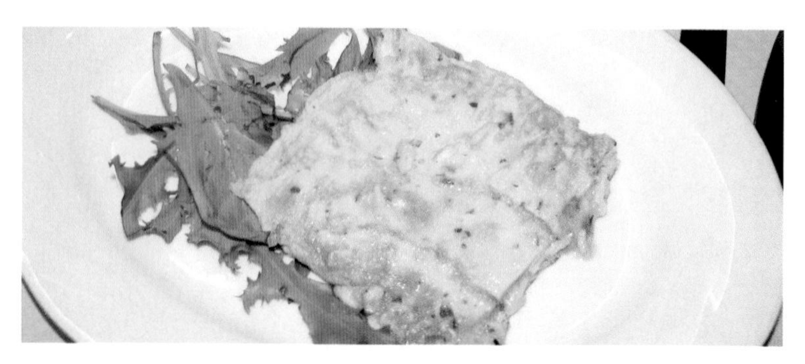

POTAGES

POUTINE SOUP (Nice, Antibes, Grasse, Cannes)

Serves 4
Preparation time: 30 mins. (including cooking)

- *5cl olive oil*
- *1 leek (finely chopped)*
- *1 onion*
- *3 cloves garlic*
- *1 tomato (peeled)*
- *3/4 litre water*
- *1 bunch sage*
- *Saffron*
- *50g grated cheese (preferably Swiss cheese)*
- *200g medium-sized poutine*
- *Salt, pepper*

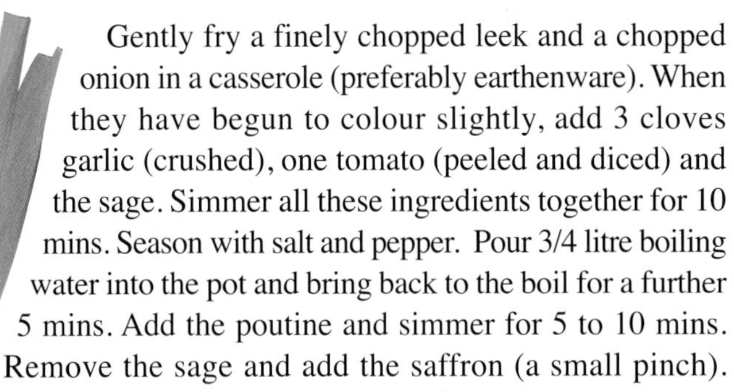

Gently fry a finely chopped leek and a chopped onion in a casserole (preferably earthenware). When they have begun to colour slightly, add 3 cloves garlic (crushed), one tomato (peeled and diced) and the sage. Simmer all these ingredients together for 10 mins. Season with salt and pepper. Pour 3/4 litre boiling water into the pot and bring back to the boil for a further 5 mins. Add the poutine and simmer for 5 to 10 mins. Remove the sage and add the saffron (a small pinch). Simmer for 5 mins. and remove from the heat. Slice up some bread. Place the grated cheese and croutons in a soup tureen and pour on the soup.

This recipe was given to me by Mr. Emile Cheval from Biot.

FISH SOUP

Serves 4
Preparation time: 1 hr.
Cooking time: at least 1 hr. on a low heat

- *1kg rock fish (rainbow wrasse, common wrasse, scorpion fish)*
- *1 large onion*
- *2 cloves garlic*
- *Thyme, bay*
- *1dsp. pastis*
- *1 good dsp. tomato puree*
- *4 dsp. olive oil*
- *1 dose real saffron*
- *1½ litres hot water*
- *4 dsp. grated Sbrinz or Fribourg cheese*
- *4 slices bread, cubed and grilled*

Gently fry the onion in a large pan with the thyme, bay, garlic and tomato puree, in 4 dsp. olive oil. Quickly rinse the fish under cold running water and add. Fry, stirring all the time with a long-handled spoon until the fish "break up" completely. If necessary, add more olive oil. Season with salt and pepper. Add 1½ litres hot water, 1 dsp. pastis and the saffron. Cover and simmer for 1hr. Strain the fish through a vegetable ricer, using a wide mesh, to obtain an almost dry residue. Bind the soup with 2 dsp. crème fraîche if it is too liquid. Serve, giving each guests some croutons and grated cheese. Rouille (cf. recipe) is an excellent accompaniment for fish soup but is not essential.

This recipe was kindly given to me by Jeannine de Vaugrente from Nice.

CHARCOAL BURNER'S SOUP (Biot)

Serves 4
Preparation time: 15 mins.
Cooking time: 1 hr.

- *2 large potatoes*
- *2 tomatoes*
- *1 onion*
- *2 cloves garlic*
- *1 sprig thyme*
- *3 dsp. olive oil*
- *50g angel hair pasta*
- *1 poached egg per person (4)*
- *1 small dry goat's cheese (grated)*
- *¾ litre water*

Gently fry the finely chopped onion, crushed garlic and tomatoes (skinned, deseeded and diced) in olive oil. Add the thyme and mix. Slice the potatoes horizontally then add the boiling salted water. When the vegetables are cooked, add the angel hair pasta. Bring to a slightly stronger boil then break in the eggs, one after the other. Serve, accompanied by grated goat's cheese.

This recipe was given to me by Magali Ghiglione from Biot.

AIGO BOULIDO "Boiled Water" (Provence)

Serves 4
Preparation time: 10 mins.
Cooking time: 10 mins.

- *1 litre water*
- *1 bay leaf*
- *1 sprig sage*
- *4 – 5 slices stale bread*
- *Olive oil*
- *50g grated Swiss cheese*
- *1 head of garlic*

Add salt to the water then bring to the boil. Add the garlic and bay leaf. Take a soup tureen and layer into it thin slices of stale bread moistened with olive oil, grated cheese and sage. Pour on the boiling stock and leave to infuse for a few moments. Serve very hot. The Aigo Boulido, which is a great classic of Provençal cooking, has given rise to the famous proverb, "L'aigo boulido sauvo la vido, au bout d'un tems tuo lei gênt" which means "Boiled water saves people's lives but after a while it kills them!"

This recipe, and the story that goes with it, were given to me by Magali Ghiglione from Biot.

B. Perrin-Chattard

PISTOU SOUP (Provence)

Serves 4
Preparation time: 40 mins.
Cooking time: 1 hr.

- *4 potatoes*
- *2 large courgettes (zucchini)*
- *300g cocos beans*
- *500g fresh white beans*
- *1 large white onion*
- *100g angel hair pasta*
- *Basil (the leaves from a good bunch of basil)*
- *5 cloves garlic*
- *2 well-ripened tomatoes*
- *½ glass olive oil*
- *100g parmesan*

photo Dufresse

Prepare the vegetables (wash, peel and dice). Pour 2½ litres salted water into a pot and bring to the boil. Add the vegetables and simmer for 40 mins. After half-an-hour, add the angel hair pasta. Place the peeled and chopped garlic, basil and tomatoes (peeled and deseeded) in a mortar.

ed. Gisserot

Gradually add some olive oil, crushing the ingredients with the pestle as you do so ("pister" en Provençal, hence the name of the soup). Finish by adding some grated cheese which should immediately be crushed with the above ingredients. Season with salt and pepper then remove from the heat and blend this mixture with the hot soup. Stir and serve.

MILK SOUP

Serves 2
Preparation time: 15 mins. (including cooking)

- *40g butter*
- *2 leeks (white parts only)*
- *2 dsp. milk*
- *1/3 litre water*
- *50g angel hair pasta*
- *Salt, pepper*
- *Grated nutmeg*

Gently fry the finely chopped leeks in the butter, using an earthenware pan. Pour in the two dessertspoons of milk and 1/3 litre water. Boil for a few minutes then add the pasta. The soup should be thick. Season with salt and pepper and add a little grated nutmeg. If liked, add a small knob of butter to the soup just before serving.

FISH

SPINACH-STUFFED SARDINES (Nice)

Serves 5
Preparation time: 35 mins.
Cooking time: 20 mins.

- *500g sardines*
- *1kg cooked spinach*
- *1 egg*
- *1 medium-sized onion*
- *Salt, pepper*
- *1 tsp. tomato puree*
- *Few pinches grated Swiss cheese*
- *1 dsp. olive oil*
- *A little bread soaked in milk (crusts removed)*

ed. Gisserot

Place a saucepan over a gentle heat and combine the spinach and chopped onion with olive oil. Season with salt and pepper. Simmer for 10 mins. Squeeze excess liquid out the bread soaked in milk and add to the mixture, with the egg. Mix well. Remove the backbone from the sardines without breaking up the fish. Spread the fish out on absorbent paper. Place the equivalent of a slightly heaped tsp. of the spinach and onion mixture on each one. Put the remaining spinach in the bottom of an oiled ovenproof dish. Roll up the stuffed sardines and lay them on the bed of spinach. Dot each fish roll with tomato puree.

Sprinkle with a little Swiss cheese and drizzle a little olive oil on each sardine. Place in a medium oven (Thermostat 5-6) for 20 mins. This traditional dish can be eaten hot or cold, depending on the season.

SARDINES A L'ESCABECHE
(Provence, coast of Var, Nice)

Serves 4
Preparation time: 30 mins. (including cooking) + 1 night

- *500g. sardines*
- *1 large onion*
- *Thyme, bay, rosemary*
- *1 clove garlic*
- *1 glass wine vinegar*
- *4 dsp. olive oil*

Remove the backbone of the sardines without breaking up the fish. Dip in flour and fry in a large pan. Set aside in a large dish. Fry the chopped onion and herbs in olive oil then carefully drizzle in some vinegar. Bring to the boil for a few minutes. Strain through a conical sieve and pour this herb-flavoured vinegar over the sardines. Leave to marinate in the fridge overnight. Serve.

B. Perrin-chattard

CONGER EEL WITH SAFFRON (Toulon)

Serves 6
Preparation time: 5 mins.
Cooking time: 40 mins.

- *1 large conger eel*
- *4 dsp. olive oil*
- *4 cloves garlic*
- *2 dsp. flour*
- *Salt, pepper*
- *Water*
- *1 bay leaf*
- *A pinch saffron*

Cut the eel into fairly thick pieces and fry in olive oil. Once golden, remove from the pan and fry the 4 cloves of garlic until golden then bind with flour to form a thick roux. Add enough water to reach halfway up the fish. Season (pepper well) and flavour with bay and a small pinch of saffron. Simmer for 10 mins. When ready, place the pieces of eel back in it and simmer for a further 10 or 15 mins. to heat the fish. Serve.

ed. Gisserot

PROVENCAL TUNA FISH (Marseille, Var)

Serves 4
Preparation time: 15 mins.
Cooking time: approx. 40 mins.

- *2 thick slices fresh tuna*
- *3 medium onions*
- *2 cloves garlic*
- *2 tomatoes*
- *1 tsp. tomato puree*
- *1 carrot*
- *1 bay leaf*
- *4 dsp. olive oil*
- *Salt, pepper*
- *1 glass white wine*

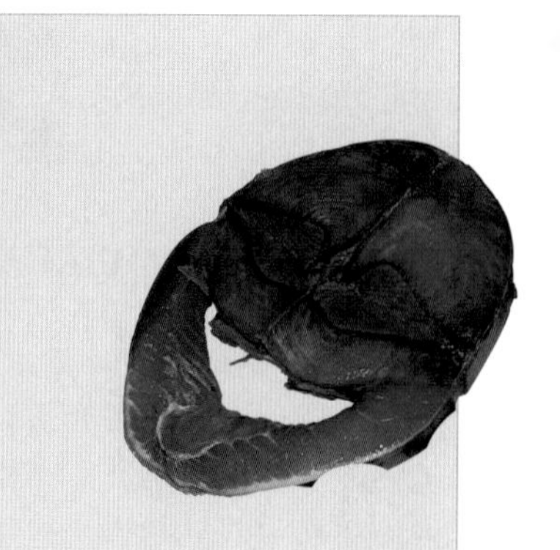

Soak the tuna fish in water containing a small quantity of vinegar. Dry with kitchen paper. Place 2 dsp. olive oil in a high-sided frying pan and, when hot, add the peeled, finely-chopped onions, garlic and tomatoes (washed, deseeded and chopped). Also add 1 carrot cut into slices and a bay leaf. Lay the tuna on top, season with salt and pepper and add 1 or 2 spoons olive oil. Cook for 5 mins. then add 1 glass white wine. Allow the alcohol to evaporate before covering the pan. Simmer over a gentle heat for 15 mins. then carefully turn the tuna over (it breaks up easily). Simmer for a further 15 mins. over a gentle heat. Just before serving, remove the bay leaf.

ed. Gisserot

ed. Gisserot

BOUILLABAISSE (Marseille)

Serves 7 at least
Preparation time: 2 hrs. (including cooking)

To make this fish stew properly, you must have as many different types of fish as possible. Rock fish are best i.e. scorpionfish (essential), wrasse, John Dory, monkfish (head only to make the stock), rainbow wrasse and conger eel.

- *2 medium- sized fish per person (or 5 slices per person)*
- *1 onion*
- *2 tomatoes*
- *3 cloves garlic*
- *1 slice lemon*
- *Fennel, bay*
- *Saffron, salt, pepper*
- *2 dsp. flour*
- *Olive oil (approx. 2 decilitres)*

Clean all the fish, taking care not to prick yourself with the scorpionfish. Using a cast-iron casserole, mix 1 thinly-sliced onion,

2 roughly chopped tomatoes and 3 lightly crushed cloves of garlic, 1 slice of lemon, 1 head of fennel and a few bayleaves. Add the fish to the casserole, season well with salt and pepper and add a pinch of saffron. Some more saffron will be added later, a few minutes before serving. Lightly dust with flour, drizzle with olive oil, stir the fish with a wooden spoon and leave to marinate for 1 hr. without covering the casserole. In a separate pan, boil enough water to cover the fish and add the monkfish and eel heads (they will be removed later). Increase the heat beneath the casserole to a maximum, after removing the softest fish. Add the boiling water (having removed the heads) and bring back to the boil for 20 mins. When everything is ready, pour the stock onto the slices of fish in a bowl. Take care not to break up the fish. Serve with rouille if liked (see recipe).

ed. Gisserot

SOUTHERN FRENCH SEA BREAM

Serves 4
Preparation time: 20 mins.
Cooking time: 20 mins.

- *1 good-sized sea bream*
- *750g ripe tomatoes*
- *½ litre dry white wine*
- *150g anchovy fillets*
- *100g large black olives (pitted)*
- *Thyme, 3 bay leaves*
- *Salt, pepper*
- *2 large onions*
- *3 dsp. olive oil*

Finely chop the onions and fry until golden in the olive oil in a high-sided frying pan. Finely chop the anchovy fillets on a board, using two knives, and the olives.

Once the onions are golden brown, add the tomatoes, anchovies and olives. Season with salt and pepper then add the 3 bay leaves and thyme. Pour on the white wine and simmer. The sauce should not be too thick. Remove the bay leaves. Place in the fish in an ovenproof dish, cover with the sauce and place in a medium oven. Bake for approximately 20 mins.

This recipe is delicious using tuna fish in place of sea bream. Marinate the fresh tuna in oil for two days in the fridge.

Recommended wine : Coteau varois, Bandol.

THON A LA MÉRIDIONALE (Nice)

Serves 4
Preparation time: 10 mins. + two days in the fridge
Cooking time: 20 mins.

2 good slices tuna
same ingredients as the sea bream recipe

For the oil marinade:
- *½ thinly-sliced fresh onion*
- *1 carrot*
- *Thyme, bay*
- *Salt, pepper*
- *Olive oil*

Place the tuna slices on a dish large enough to be able to lay them flat, side by side. Cover with ½ thinly-sliced onion, a sliced carrot, thyme and bay (3 or 4 leaves). Season with salt and pepper. Cover the fish with olive oil and place in the refrigerator for 24 hours. Turn the slices in the marinade and leave for a further 24 hours in the refrigerator. The marinade is then removed before baking the fish in the oven, covered with the tomato and olive sauce described in the previous recipe. It can be eaten hot or cold.

This recipe has been kindly given to me by Jeannine de Vaugrente.

PROVENCAL-STYLE PRAWNS (Nice, Var coast)

Serves 4
Preparation time: 20 mins.
Cooking time: 15 mins.

- *12 king prawns*
- *1 medium-sized onion*
- *1 carrot*
- *3 dsp. olive oil*
- *½ glass cognac*
- *1 glass dry white wine*
- *2 tsp. tomato puree*
- *1 bouquet garni (thyme, bay leaf, parsley)*
- *Salt, Cayenne pepper*
- *½ clove garlic*

photo Dufresse

photo Dufresse

Put a finely chopped onion and carrot in a high-sided frying pan. Fry gently in a few spoons of olive oil then add the prawns, turning them quickly so that they turn red. Pour in half-a-glass of cognac and flambé. Add a glass of dry white wine, 1 or 2 tsp. tomato puree and a bouquet garni. Season with salt and add a good pinch of Cayenne pepper. Taste and if it is not spicy enough, add some more Cayenne pepper. Simmer for 10 mins. Remove the bouquet garni, dot with the chopped ½ clove of garlic and serve piping hot.

BOURRIDE (Provence)

Serves 7 or 8
Preparation time: 30 mins.
Cooking time: 20 mins.

This traditional dish is made only with white fish (monkfish, sea bass, whiting). This is the difference between a bourride and a bouillabaisse. It requires approximately 1½ kg fish.

- *½ monkfish*
- *1 sea bass*
- *½ whiting*
- *1 thinly-sliced onion*
- *Thyme, fennel, bay*
- *1 egg yolk per person*
- *12 slices bread*
- *Aïoli sauce (see recipe)*

ed. Gisserot

Cut the fish into pieces and lay in a casserole with the thinly-sliced onion, thyme and bay. Cover the fish with hot water. Season with salt and pepper and simmer for approximately 15 mins. Meanwhile, place the slices of stale bread in a dish to form a layer 1 centimetre thick. When the fish is cooked, pour some stock over the bread without soaking it too much. Use some of the aïoli (the remainder will be served in a sauceboat). Allow 2 dsp. aïoli and one egg yolk per person. Pour on the fish stock and stir well. Put back over a low heat and, using a wooden spoon, stir until thickened, as if you were making custard. The sauce has the right texture when it totally coats the wooden spoon. Immediately remove from the heat and pour it over the bread. Serve the fish and the remainder of the aïoli separately.

Recommended wine: red Bandol.

LEG OF LAMB WITH GARLIC MASH

Serves 6
Preparation time: 15 mins.
Cooking time: 15 mins. per lb.

- *1 leg lamb*
- *12 cloves garlic*
- *Olive oil*
- *Sea salt*
- *Pepper*

Rub the leg of lamb with sea salt, cut slits in the meat and push in some garlic then roast. While the lamb is roasting, cook a dozen cloves of garlic in a little olive oil over a gentle heat. When the garlic is well cooked, mash it with a fork and soften it with some olive oil over a gentle heat. Gradually add the cooking liquor from the meat, season if necessary then serve in a sauceboat as an accompaniment to the meat.

This recipe was given to me by Madame Bodet (Cuers).

photo Dufresse

POULET AU CITRON (Nice)

Serves 4 or 5
Preparation time: 15 mins.
Cooking time: 20 mins.

- *1 chicken*
- *2 lemons*
- *1 whole onion*
- *1 egg*
- *Salt, pepper*
- *Sunflower oil*
- *1 large knob butter*
- *Medium-grain couscous (2 glasses)*

Fry the thinly-sliced onion over a low heat in a mixture of oil and butter in a pressure cooker. Add the chicken and turn over several times without allowing it to colour. Season with salt and pepper. Cut 2 or 3 slices of lemon and add to the pressure cooker. Pour in enough water to reach halfway up the chicken; any more would produce a stew. Close the pressure cooker and cook over a medium heat for 15 to 20 mins. after the cooker begins to hiss. The chicken should be well cooked. Remove the meat from the pan and strain the jus through a sieve. Press through as much as possible, using the back of a wooden spoon. When ready to serve, bind the jus with an egg, stirring all the time over a low heat. Add the juice of 1 lemon and pour the sauce over the chicken just before serving.

This recipe was given to me by Madame Jeannine de Vaugrente (Nice).

STUFFED VEAL (Provence, Nice)

Serves 4
Preparation time: 45 mins.
Cooking time: 1 hr.

- *1 piece of veal (get your butcher to form a pouch)*
- *1 small glass rice*
- *1 bunch Swiss chard (leaves only)*
- *4 medium slices ham*
- *Same weight of cooked, minced veal*
- *2 or 3 slices smoked bacon (finely chopped)*
- *1 clove garlic*
- *1 egg*
- *Salt, pepper*
- *1 small handful bread soaked in milk*
- *50g grated cheese (Parmesan or Sbrinz)*
- *A selection of vegetables (as if making a stew)*

Cook the rice. Mix all the other ingredients i.e. cooked chard leaves, ham, minced roast veal, bacon, chopped garlic, egg and the bread (crusts removed) lightly soaked in milk. Mix the cooked rice with this stuffing and fill the "pouch" in the veal.

photo Dufresse

Stitch up with a meat needle and twine. Cook the pouch in lightly salted cold water (do not use too much salt because the stuffing ingredients are already salted), with the vegetables. Prick the meat with a fork to see if it is cooked then drain it and allow it to brown in the oven, adding some butter on top. The stuffed veal is best eaten cold because it is almost impossible to cut while still hot.

This recipe was given to me by Madame Broc of Nice.

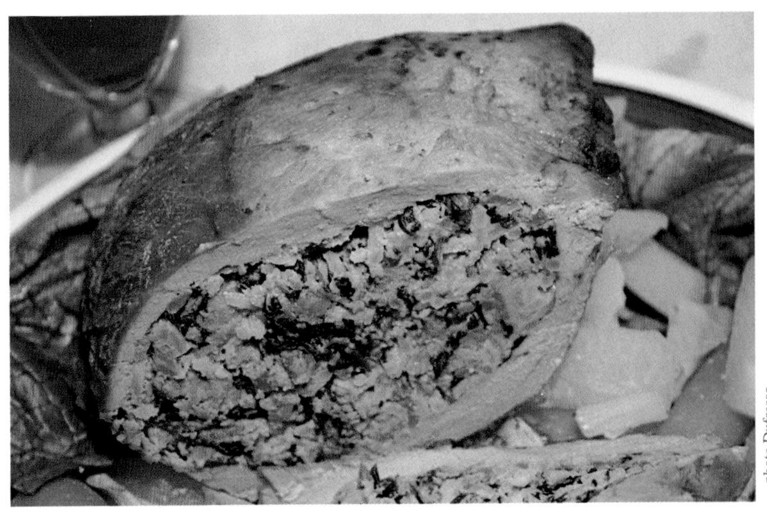

photo Dufresse

AILLADE (Cuers, Pierrefeu)

«Aiado »
Serves 4
Preparation time: 10 mins.
Cooking time: 1 hr. 10 mins.

- *Pieces of veal 5 cms. long (cut from the rump)*
- *4 dsp. olive oil*
- *Stale breadcrumbs (1 dsp.)*
- *10 cloves garlic*
- *3 tomatoes (chopped)*
- *Salt, pepper*
- *1 glass white wine*

Cut the rump into pieces approx. 5 cms. long and fry in oil until golden brown. Remove them from the pan and fry 1 dsp. of fine crumbs made from stale bread, 10 cloves of garlic (peeled) and 3 chopped tomatoes. Season with salt and pepper and add 1 glass of white wine. Simmer for approximately 20 mins. then put the meat back in the sauce. Simmer for a further 45 mins. then serve.

This recipe was given to me by Madame Bodet (Cuers).

BOILED BEEF (Provence)

Serves 6
Preparation time: 15 mins.
Cooking time: 4 hrs. (or 2½ in a pressure cooker)

- *800g beef (short ribs)*
- *800g lean beef*
- *1 good-sized marrow bone*
- *1/2 calf's foot*
- *5 medium-sized carrots (no more than this or the stew will be slightly sweet)*
- *3 medium-sized leeks*
- *3 or 4 turnips*
- *1 very small bunch celery*
- *1 piece marrow or cabbage*
- *1 good-sized onion stuck with two cloves*

On the evening before you cook the boiled beef, wrap the meat and marrow bone in gauze and place in a large stewpan (preferably earthenware) filled with water. Do not add salt. Bring the pan to the boil and simmer for 1 hr. Remove from the heat and place in a cool place overnight (not necessarily in the refrigerator). The next day, skim off any fat that has formed on the top. Reheat the pan until the stock begins to boil and add all the vegetables. It is easier to tie the leeks into a bunch; this prevents them from splitting into string-like pieces in the pot. Season with salt and pepper. Simmer over a low heat for at least 3 hrs. Remove the onion and discard it. Once boiled, it becomes bland but it will have given off all its flavour into the stew while cooking. If cooking the stew in a pressure cooker, simmer for 1 hr on the previous evening without the lid then, the next day, seal the lid and cook the stew for 1½ hrs. only.

photo J-P. Gisserot

NICE-STYLE RABBIT

Serves 6
Preparation time: 20 mins.
Cooking time: 45 mins. to 1 hr. depending on the size of the rabbit

- *1 rabbit (1.5 to 1.8 kg), cut into pieces*
- *1.5 decilitres olive oil*
- *1 large onion*
- *2 cloves garlic*
- *6 tomatoes*
- *3 courgettes (zucchini)*
- *1 aubergine (eggplant)*
- *A few black olives*
- *Thyme, rosemary*

photo Dufresse

Ask your butcher to cut the rabbit into pieces. Brown them in a round casserole with half the olive oil. When they are well browned, season with salt and pepper then add the finely chopped onion, some thyme and rosemary. Sweat the onion for 5 mins. Meanwhile, peel the tomatoes, remove the seeds and crush them roughly. Add them to the casserole with the cloves of garlic (crushed with a pestle and mortar) and steam for a few moments. Peel the courgettes and cut into large cubes. Wash the aubergine (without peeling it) and cut into thick half-slices. Fry quickly in a frying pan with the remainder of the olive oil and add all the vegetables to the casserole. Cover and place in the oven until fully cooked. Check the seasoning and add more if required. Serve in the casserole, decorated with a few black olives.

POULTRY RISOTTO

Serves 4
Preparation time: 10 mins.
Cooking time: 30 mins.

- *150g white rice*
- *3 dsp. olive oil*
- *2 red peppers (capsicum) or a tin of peppers*
- *1 medium-sized onion*
- *Remains of roast chicken or turkey*
- *Curry powder*
- *Hot water*

This dish, which can be served as a main course, is a useful way of using up left-overs from roast chicken.

Fry a thinly-sliced onion in 2 dsp. olive oil in a high-sided frying pan. When the onion is golden, add the remainder of the oil and the rice (washed). Stir to prevent the rice from sticking and cook for 5 mins. Then add the hot water, a little at a time, letting the onion and rice absorb it before adding some more. Monitor the rice and add water as necessary, remembering to season with salt and pepper. Finally, sprinkle with enough curry powder to give the rice a delicious yellow colour. Meanwhile, cut the peppers into strips no more than 3 cm in length, on a chopping board. Do likewise with the chicken. When the rice is almost cooked, mix in the peppers and chicken. Finish cooking, check the seasoning and serve piping hot.

If the capsicums are fresh, cook them slightly in a separate saucepan, otherwise they may not be sufficiently cooked.

photo Dufresse

PROVENCAL BEEF STEW (Nice)

Serves 4 to 5
Preparation time: 30 mins. + overnight
Cooking time: 3 hrs in a stewpot

- 800g to 1 kg stewing beef
(slightly gelatinous but not too fibrous)
- 1 piece pork rind
- 1 dsp. flour

marinade :
- 1 litre red wine (minimum)
- 1 beef stock cube diluted in a bowl of hot water
- 2 dsp. olive oil
- 1 onion
- 1 clove garlic
- Thyme, bay, pepper (no salt)

photo Dufresse

Chop the meat into large cubes (approximately 60 cm). Marinate in enough red wine to cover the meat, with the olive oil, sliced onion, finely-chopped garlic, thyme and bay. Season with pepper. Leave to marinate overnight in a cool place or for 48 hours in the refrigerator (not recommended). When it is time to cook the meat, lay a piece of pork rind in the bottom of a stewpot. Drain the meat and wipe with absorbent paper. Dust lightly with flour and pour in two-thirds of the marinade. Add the bowl of stock. Now season with salt. Place the lid on the stewpot and simmer for at least 3 hours over a gentle heat. This recipe can be made in a pressure cooker, in which case cooking time will be reduced to 1½ hours. Provençal stew, a dish full of flavour, can be kept for several days and gently reheated before each meal. It is also popular, eaten with pasta or polenta (see recipe).

ESCALE
MUCHACHA
La Rhumerie
PIZZERIA
RESTAURANT

PANISSES (Marseille, Nice)

Serves 6
Preparation time: 10 mins.
Cooking time: 20 mins. then 2 mins. to cool

- *1 litre water*
- *1 large pinch salt*
- *2 dsp. olive oil*
- *250g chickpea meal or cornflour*

Pour 1 litre water into a pan with a large pinch of salt and 2 dsp. olive oil. Bring to the boil and immediately remove from the heat. Pour the 250g chickpea meal or cornflour into the water, avoiding the formation of lumps (if lumps do form, pour the mix into a blender to smooth then continue with the recipe). Use a large wooden spoon to mix the flour or meal well into the water. Place the pan back over the heat and thicken the mixture for 15 to 20 mins, gently stirring all the time. Once the "boiled meal" is ready, pour it onto lightly oiled saucers. This must be done quickly and accurately because the dough cools quickly and cannot then be moulded by the saucer.

FRIED PANISSES (Nice)

Serves 6
Preparation time: 5 mins.
Cooking time: 2 to 3 mins. per panisse

Prepare the panisses as above then cut them out as if making chips. This requires care as panisses are more fragile than raw potatoes. They should not be more than 1 cm (1/2 inch) thick. Heat some oil in a deep fat fryer until boiling then fry the panisses for 2 mins. until golden brown and crisp. Carefully remove from the fryer because they break even when cooked. The panisses can then be sprinkled with salt or, even better, with sugar. If sugar is used, they are a meal to themselves.

ed. Gisserot

SOCCA (Nice)

Serves 6
Preparation time: 10 mins.
Cooking time: 10 mins.

- *250g chickpea meal*
- *½ glass olive oil*
- *Salted boiling water*
- *1 pinch salt*
- *Pepper*

Mix 250g chickpea meal with the boiling water. Add ½ glass olive oil. Cook over a gentle heat until thickened. Pour onto an oiled cake tin base and bake in a hot oven for 10 mins. Serve hot with a good amount of pepper.

ed. Gisserot

GNOCCHIS (Nice)

Serves 6
Preparation time: 15 mins.
Cooking time: 20 mins.

- *¼ litre water*
- *100g butter*
- *1 pinch salt*
- *125g flour*
- *100g grated Swiss cheese*
- *4 eggs*
- *Nutmeg*
- *Pepper*
- *100g boiled potatoes (optional)*

Bring to the boil the ¼ litre water, 100g butter and pinch of salt. Once boiling, add 125g flour, remove from the heat and mix well with a wooden spoon. Place the pan back on the heat and beat hard continuously to prevent the dough from sticking. Remove from the heat and beat in the eggs, half the grated cheese, the nutmeg and pepper.

photo Dufresse

photo Dufresse

At this point, you can add 100g potatoes (boiled in their skins and peeled when cooked). Spoon out quantities of dough no bigger than a quail's egg and place in a large pan of boiling salted water. Remove the gnocchi as soon as they float to the surface. Place them in a gratin dish and cover with the remainder of the grated cheese. Season with salt and pepper and bake in the oven for approximately 15 minutes.

CANNELLONIS (Nice)

Serves 4
Preparation time: 30 mins.
Cooking time: 50 mins. (20 mins. + 15 mins. + 15 mins.)

- *1 packet dry cannelloni*
  (it is time-consuming and rather difficult to prepare the dough so it is better to buy it ready for use)
- *1 bunch Swiss chard (leaves only)*
- *1 onion (chopped)*
- *Small handful of bread soaked in milk*
  (remove crusts first)
- *1 egg*
- *Left-over boiled or casseroled beef*
- *Salt, pepper*
- *1 dsp. groundnut or sunflower oil*
- *Fairly liquid tomato sauce*
- *100g grated Swiss cheese*

photo Dufresse

Place the cannelloni in a large pan of boiling salted water and cook for 10 mins, adding 1 dsp. oil to prevent the cannelloni sticking to each other. Once cooked, carefully remove them from the pan with a strainer so as not to break them. Lay them side by side on a clean, dry cloth and set aside. Cook the chard leaves in boiling water (5 – 10 mins.) then drain. Cut the leaves with two pairs of scissors. Cook all the ingredients for the stuffing together for approximately 15 mins. then season with salt and pepper. Using a dessertspoon, place some stuffing on each cannelloni, roll up and place in an oiled gratin dish. Cover with tomato sauce and grated cheese. Sprinkle with olive oil and bake in the oven for 15 mins.

You can buy precooked cannelloni in the shape of tubes. Use them if you can because they avoid the difficult task of cooking the pasta.

photo Dufresse

PIZZA (Nice)

Serves 4
Preparation time: 15 mins.
Cooking time: 20 mins.

- *10 heaped dsp. flour*
- *4 dsp. powdered milk*
- *3 dsp. oil (ground nut or sunflower)*
- *1 level tsp. baking powder*
- *1 large pinch salt*
- *Warm water*
- *1 tin peeled tomatoes*
- *Oregano*
- *A handful of black Nice olives*
- *A sachet of grated parmesan*
- *Salt, pepper*
- *Olive oil*

photo Dufresse

Make a dough with the flour, salt, baking powder, powdered milk and sunflower oil, adding the equivalent of 3 dsp. warm water to get the right consistency. Spread the dough out in a well-oiled fluted round cake tin. Decorate with the peeled tomatoes, removing as much juice as possible. Sprinkle thickly with oregano and grated parmesan then add some local black olives. Season well with pepper. Drizzle on some olive oil in a circular motion. Bake in a preheated moderate oven (Thermostat 7) for 20 mins. This home-made pizza recipe is easy and quick and the pizza can be eaten hot, as a main course, or cold on the following day as a starter or cut into thin slivers and served with an aperitif.

POLENTA (County of Nice)

Serves 5
Preparation time: 40 mins. (including cooking)

- *2½ litres water*
- *500g cornflour*
- *2 tsp. salt*

Gradually pour 500g cornflour into 2½ litres boiling salted water, taking care not to form lumps. Stir constantly with a wooden spoon for thirty minutes, over a low heat. This filling dish is traditionally served with a beef casserole.

N. Martinez

STEAMED COURGETTES (Hinterland of Nice)

Serves 4
Preparation time: 10 mins.
Cooking time: 25 mins.

- *5 medium-sized courgettes (zucchini)*
- *2 finely chopped onions*
- *2 cloves garlic*
- *Thyme, rosemary*
- *5 cl olive oil*
- *Salt, pepper*
- *75g Swiss cheese or Comté (grated)*

In a large deep-sided frying pan, fry the finely chopped onions and chopped cloves of garlic in oil (one-half of the amount indicated). The onions and garlic should not be allowed to colour; they should become transparent (7 mins. maximum). Meanwhile, wash the courgettes, remove the ends and, without peeling them, cut them horizontally into slices 5mm thick. Add the courgettes and the remainder of the oil to the onion and garlic mixture. Sprinkle with the herbs and stir to distribute the fat evenly through the vegetables. Season with salt and pepper. Simmer the vegetables for 10 mins. over a moderate heat, without covering the pan. Check to ensure that the courgettes are not sticking to the pan then cover. If necessary, add a small quantity of olive oil (no more than 1 dsp). Simmer over a gentle heat for 10 mins. Check the seasoning then turn off the heat. Sprinkle the grated cheese over the vegetables while still hot. As soon as the cheese has melted (3 or 4 mins.), serve.

This recipe was kindly given to me by Mrs. Grassi (l'Escosène).

COURGETTE FLOWERS IN BATTER (Nice)

Serves 3
Preparation time: 10 mins.
Cooking time: 10 mins.

- *1 bunch courgette (zucchini) flowers*
- *1 egg*
- *6 dsp. flour*
- *1 small glass water*
- *1 dsp. groundnut oil for the pan (+ 1 drop for the batter)*
- *1 glass warm water*
- *Salt, pepper*

Wash the floweres, discarding the tails and the green corolla. Lay them on absorbent kitchen paper. Make a very liquid batter with the flour, egg, 1 drop oil and water. Add a pinch of salt. Dip the flowers in the batter and place in a pan containing boiling oil. Turn them as soon as the batter has cooked. The batter should be golden but not brown. Sprinkle with salt and serve immediately.

ed. Gisserot

COURGETTE AND RICE TIAN

Serves 4
Preparation time: 20 mins.
Cooking time: 10 mins.

- *1 kg courgettes (zucchini)*
- *1 small onion (chopped)*
- *3 eggs*
- *50g Swiss cheese (grated)*
- *1 glass rice*
- *Salt, pepper*

Wash the courgettes and cut into pieces 5cm long. Cook for 5 mins. in boiling water. Wash the rice separately and cook in cold water. If it is "quick boil" rice, simmer for 10 mins; otherwise it will take 20 mins. to cook. Separate the egg. Set the whites aside in a tall container. Mix the cooked courgettes, cooked rice, egg yolks and chopped onion together in a basin. Season with salt and pepper. Beat the egg whites until they form stiff peaks then delicately fold them into the courgette mixture with a wooden spoon. Butter an ovenproof dish and pour in the mixture. Sprinkle with grated cheese and bake in a medium oven (Thermostat 5) for 10 mins. until golden. This gratin can be served hot but it is also very tasty as a cold dish, especially in the summer. Cooked, finely-chopped Swiss chard leaves can also be added to the courgette and rice mixture.

COURGETTE, RICE AND TOMATO TIAN

Serves 4 or 5
Preparation time: 1 hr. (including cooking)

- *1 large onion*
- *1 kg large courgettes (zucchini)*
- *1 small glass rice*
- *1 dsp. tomato puree*
- *50g grated cheese*
- *Salt, pepper*
- *2 dsp. groundnut oil*

Fry the chopped onion gently in oil in a high-sided frying pan. When it is golden, add the tomato puree then the courgettes, peeled and sliced. Cook over a gentle heat until the courgettes can be mashed with a fork. Season with salt and pepper. Cook the rice in lightly salted water. Add the cooked rice to the courgette – onion – tomato mixture. If necessary, add a little hot water. Mix with half the grated cheese and pour into a buttered ovenproof dish. Sprinkle the remainder of the cheese on top and bake in the oven for 10 mins. until golden.

ed. Gisserot

AUBERGINE TIAN (Provence)

Serves 4
Preparation time: 20 mins.
Cooking time: 25 mins.

- *3 large aubergines (eggplants)*
- *Herbs*
- *Salt, pepper*
- *1 tin tomato sauce*
- *4 eggs*
- *Breadcrumbs*
- *4 dsp. groundnut or sunflower oil*
- *100g grated cheese (Swiss cheese or parmesan)*

Cut each aubergine into thin slices without peeling. Lay in a dish, cover with salt and allow them to disgorge their water then rinse carefully. Add a good quantity of herbs (oregano, thyme) and pepper (optional) to the ready-prepared tomato sauce. Dip the aubergines in the beaten eggs then in the breadcrumbs. Fry in a hot pan containing 3 dsp. oil (if necessary, you can add another 2 dsp. oil to the pan during cooking). Place a layer of aubergines in an ovenproof dish and cover with a layer of tomato sauce and a layer of cheese. Repeat three or four times. Cover the entire dish with two beaten eggs and place in the oven until golden brown.

PROVENCAL AUBERGINES

Serves 4
Preparation time: 45 mins. including cooking

- *1 large onion*
- *1 kg large courgettes (zucchini)*
- *1 small glass rice*
- *1 dsp. tomato puree*
- *50g grated cheese*
- *Salt, pepper*
- *2 dsp. groundnut oil*

Fry the chopped onion gently in oil in a high-sided frying pan. When it is golden, add the tomato puree then the courgettes, peeled and sliced. Cook over a gentle heat until the courgettes can be mashed with a fork. Season with salt and pepper. Cook the rice in lightly salted water. Add the cooked rice to the courgette – onion – tomato mixture. If necessary, add a little hot water. Mix with half the grated cheese and pour into a buttered ovenproof dish. Sprinkle the remainder of the cheese on top and bake in the oven for 10 mins. until golden.

photo Dufresse

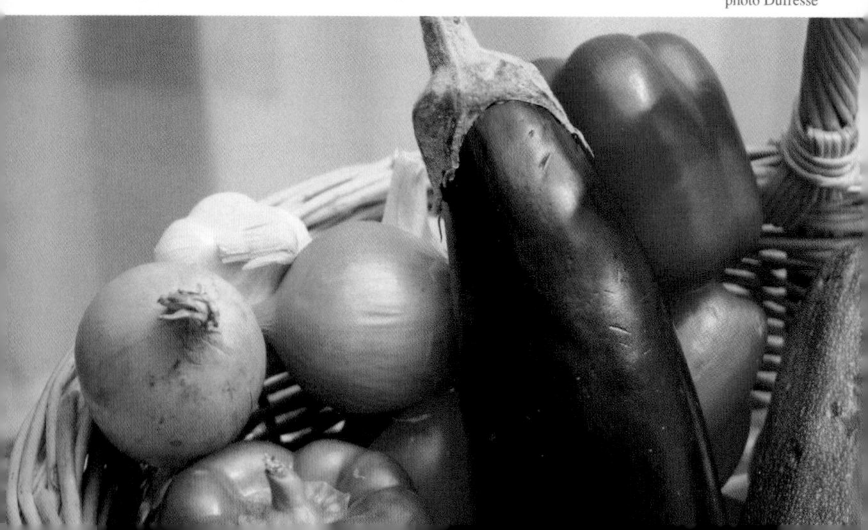

ŒUFS AUX AUBERGINES (Nice)

Serves 6
Preparation time: 15 mins.
Cooking time: 30 mins.

- *6 medium-sized aubergines (eggplants)*
- *2 shallots*
- *1 clove garlic*
- *6cl olive oil*
- *6 eggs*
- *60g grated Swiss cheese*
- *1 sprig fresh basil*
- *Salt, pepper*

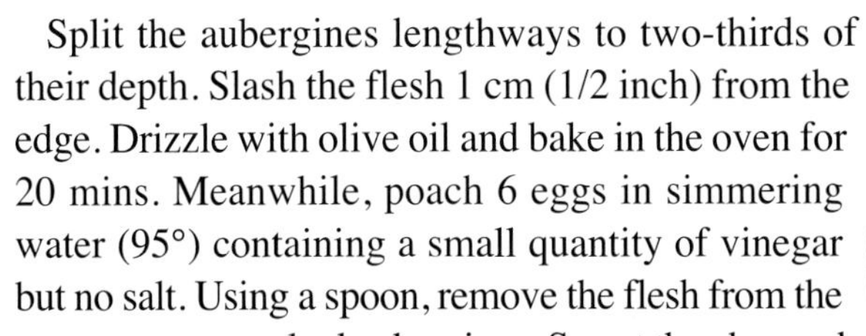

Split the aubergines lengthways to two-thirds of their depth. Slash the flesh 1 cm (1/2 inch) from the edge. Drizzle with olive oil and bake in the oven for 20 mins. Meanwhile, poach 6 eggs in simmering water (95°) containing a small quantity of vinegar but no salt. Using a spoon, remove the flesh from the cooked aubergines. Sweat the chopped shallots in 5cl olive oil (i.e. cook them without allowing them to colour). Add the aubergine flesh, crushed garlic and some chopped basil. Cook for 10 mins. Season with salt and pepper. Place an egg in each aubergine, with the cooked flesh. Sprinkle with grated cheese and brown under the grill.

SPINACH TIAN (Provence)

Serves 4
Preparation time: 30 mins.
(or 10 mins. if using ready-prepared spinach)
Cooking time: 30 mins.

- *3 kg spinach (450g if frozen)*
- *2 eggs*
- *2dl olive oil*
- *2 cloves garlic*
- *50gr breadcrumbs*
- *Salt, pepper*

Sort and wash the spinach. Drain (this is not necessary if you are using frozen spinach). Roughly chop the spinach. Using a high-sided frying pan, gently fry the two cloves of garlic (roughly crushed with a pestle and mortar) in 1 1/2 dsp. olive oil. Leave to cool. Pour the eggs over the spinach and place in a lightly-oiled ovenproof dish (known in Provençal as a “tian"). Sprinkle with breadcrumbs, drizzle on some olive oil and bake in the oven for 10 to 12 mins. until golden. If using frozen spinach, reduce the quantity of oil used (e.g. a total of 1 dl).

NICE-STYLE RATATOUILLE (Nice)

Serves 6
Preparation time: 2½ hrs. including cooking

- *2 large aubergines (eggplants)*
- *3 courgettes*
- *2 medium-sized onions*
- *1 large tin peeled tomatoes*
- *2 large peppers (capsicum), red or green*
- *1 dl olive oil*

Using a high-sided frying pan, cook the onions until golden in a small quantity of olive oil. Set aside. Cook the courgettes until golden then add them to the onions. Set aside. Do the same for the peppers, which should be diced but not skinned. In a different pan, fry the aubergines, diced but not peeled. Once all the vegetables

ed. Gisserot

photo Dufresse

are cooked, heat them together. The tomatoes can be cooked without any fat in a frying pan until all the juice has evaporated. Add the tomatoes to the remainder of the mixture and simmer for 30 mins. Check the seasoning. A clove of garlic cut into two or three can be added to the tomatoes but is not essential. A ratatouille can be eaten hot but it is even better, served cold.

PROVENCAL TOMATOES (Provence)

Serves 4
Preparation time: 5 mins.
Cooking time: 10 mins.

- *4 medium-sized tomatoes*
- *Herbes de Provence (thyme, rosemary)*
- *1 clove garlic (chopped)*
- *1 onion (finely chopped)*
- *2 dsp. olive oil*
- *Salt, pepper*

Cut the tomatoes in half crossways. Remove as much juice as possible by shaking them over the sink. Heat the olive oil in a large frying pan and add the finely chopped onion and garlic. Place the tomato halves upside down in the pan after sprinkling them with herbs. Leave them to cook for 5 mins. over a high heat. Turn them. Heat well for a further 5 mins. Season with salt and pepper and serve hot.

ed. Gisserot

PROVENCAL TOMATOES WITH EGG (Provence)

Serves 4
Preparation time: 5 mins.
Cooking time: 20 mins.

- *4 tomatoes*
- *4 eggs*
- *Herbes de Provence*
- *1 clove garlic (chopped)*
- *1 onion (finely chopped)*
- *2 dsp. olive oil*
- *Salt, pepper*

Prepare the tomatoes as in the previous recipe but, when they are cooked, break the eggs between the tomato halves. Cook until the egg whites have set. Serve.

Cl. Perrin-Chattard

ARTICHOKES A LA BARIGOULE (Provence)

Serves 4
Preparation time: 20 mins.
Cooking time: 45 mins.

- *4 artichokes*
- *3 dsp. olive oil*
- *1 medium onion*
- *2 carrots*
- *Salt, pepper*
- *1 small glass white wine*
- *2 cloves garlic*
- *Water*

Remover a few leaves from the artichokes and level up some of the others. Put 3 dsp. olive oil in a pan with the chopped onion and 2 raw, finely diced carrots. Lay the artichokes on top with the leaves pointing upwards. Season with salt and pepper. Drizzle on some oil, cover the pan and heat over a moderate heat, stirring occasionally. As soon as the onion and carrots begin to brown, pour in a glass of white wine and allow to reduce by one-half. Add 2 cloves of garlic and a few spoons of water then simmer over a low heat. Pour the sauce over the artichokes and serve.

ARTICHOKES A LA BARIGOULE 2 (Biot)

Serves 4
Preparation time: 30 mins.
Cooking time: Approx. 1 hr

- *12 small local purple artichokes*
- *500g white or brown onions*
- *3 dsp. olive oil*
- *2 or 3 cloves garlic*
- *1 bunch parsley*
- *12 thin slices streaky bacon*
- *40g butter*

Cut off the top of the artichoke leaves then remove the hardest leaves and the choke. Scoop out the heart slightly. In a basin, mix the softened butter with the chopped parsley, pressed garlic, salt and pepper. Fill the artichoke hearts with the mixture then roll each artichoke in a slice of streaky bacon. Put some olive oil in a casserole (2 or 3 dsp) with the chopped onions. Allow the onions to go golden before adding the artichokes. Leave for 5 to 10 mins. until golden. Add two small ladles of water to the pan, cover, lower the heat to a minimum and simmer for 30 to 40 mins, checking occasionally to make sure they are not sticking to the pan. Before the end of the cooking time, add some chopped parsley, stir and serve piping hot.

This recipe was given to me by Magali Ghiglione from Biot.

ed. Gisserot

STUFFED VEGETABLES (Provence, Nice, Grasse)

Serves 6
Preparation time: 1 hr.
Cooking time: 30 to 45 mins.

- 8 courgettes (zucchini)
- 4 large white onions
- 3 large aubergines (eggplants)
- 4 yellow or red peppers (capsicums)
- 4 medium tomatoes
- 4 slices medium-sliced ham (1)
(1) Same weight of roast veal or pork (cooked and minced)
- 2 or 3 slices smoky bacon
cut into very small pieces but not minced
- 1 clove garlic
- 1 egg
- Parsley, pepper, salt
- A small handful of bread soaked in milk (remove crusts)
- 100g grated cheese (Sbrinz or parmesan)

photo Dufresse

Wash the vegetables and blanch the courgettes and onions in salted boiling water (the aubergines, peppers and tomatoes do not require prior cooking). Remove "caps" from the vegetables, except the aubergines which should be cut in two lengthways. Scoop out the flesh from all the vegetables and lay them face downwards on the grill pan. The flesh should, of course, be kept and mixed with the stuffing and cheese. Tomatoes are best set out in a separate pan because, even if laid face down under the grill and wiped with absorbent kitchen paper, they still give off some liquid while cooking. To overcome this, place a few grains of dry rice in the bottom of the pan; it will swell and absorb any excess juice. Place all the vegetables on a shelf in the oven. Make the stuffing by mixing the ham, roast veal (or pork), flesh from the vegetables, grated cheese, egg, bread soaked in milk, parsley and finely chopped garlic in a bowl. Season moderately with salt and pepper because the meat will already be salted. Fill the vegetables with the stuffing and add a small knob of butter on top. Put the "caps" back on the tomatoes and courgettes then bake in a medium oven for 30 to 45 minutes. The stuffed vegetables freeze very well if you use only fresh ingredients. However, they should be separated from each other by being wrapped in aluminium foil.

This recipe was given to me by Mrs. Broc from Nice.

ed. Gisserot

NICE OLIVES

Preparation time: 5 mins.
Storage time: several weeks

- *500g Nice olives*
- *3 clean jam jars with lids*
- *1 dsp. fine table salt*
- *Cold water*

Buy 500g Nice olives at the market. Mix the salt with the water in a bowl and put the olives in jars. Cover with salted water and seal the jars well.

photo Dufresse

PEPPERS IN OLIVE OIL

Preparation time: 20 mins.
Cooking time: 1 hr.

- *4 large peppers (capsicum), red or green*
- *Olive oil*

Split the peppers in two and remove the small seeds inside. Halve them again and lay them on a grid placed midway up the oven. Grill the peppers under a very gentle heat until their skin becomes black and cracked. Turn off the heat and carefully remove the peppers from the grill. Run them under warm water, one by one, to remove the skin. There should not be any black flecks left on the peppers because this spoils their flavour. Lay the strips of pepper in a salad bowl and drizzle on a good amount of olive oil. Prepared in this way, the peppers can be kept for several days outside the refrigerator. If you place them in the fridge, the oil may become opaque. To revive the appetising appearance of the peppers, leave them at ambient temperature for a few minutes.

ed. Gisserot

ANCHOVY SAUCE (Nice area)

Serves 5
Preparation time: 20 mins.
No cooking required

- *5 anchovies*
- *2 cloves garlic*
- *1 egg yolk*
- *1 dsp. cold water*
- *¼ litre olive oil*
- *Lemon juice*
- *Pepper*

ed. Gisserot

Remove the salt from the anchovies and cut into small pieces. Remove the skin from the garlic and chop into small pieces. Blend these ingredients with a pestle and mortar. Add the cold water and egg yolk and beat as if making mayonnaise. This sauce goes very well with a fondue or poached white fish.

ANCHOVY BUTTER (Provence)

Serves 5
Preparation time: 15 mins.
No cooking required

- *6 or 8 anchovies*
- *250g butter*
- *1 lemon (juice only)*

Remove the salt from the anchovies and blend to a fine paste with a pestle and mortar. Mix with the slightly softened butter (do not soften it too much!). Add the juice of 1 lemon and mix again. Do not put the anchovy butter in the fridge before serving. It is usually served on small slices of toast, as an aperitif.

ed. Gisserot

ROUILLE (Martigues, Marseille, Aix)

Preparation time: 15 mins.
Served with bouillabaisse

- *2 cloves garlic*
- *½ pimento (chilli)*
- *Handful of bread soaked in milk (remove crusts)*
- *1 dl. olive oil*
- *2 or 3 potatoes cooked in the bouillabaisse*
- *2 spoons stock*

ed. Gisserot

Using a pestle and mortar, crush the 2 cloves of garlic, half a pimento and some bread soaked in milk. Bind with olive oil. Crush 3 potatoes with the remainder of the oil and, to finish, make the saucer lighter by adding 2 or 3 spoons of stock. Serve with a bouillabaisse.

AIOLI (Provence)

Serves 6
Preparation time: 25 mins.

- *6 to 10 cloves garlic to taste (between ½ and 2 per person)*
- *1 egg yolk*
- *1 pinch salt*
- *¼ to ½ litre olive oil at room temperature*
- *1 lemon (juice only)*
- *Warm water*

Peel the cloves of garlic and mash to a paste with a pestle and mortar. Add a pinch of salt and an egg yolk then pour in the oil very slowly, mixing all the time to produce a thick cream. Then add the lemon juice and 1 to 2 tsp. warm water (this prevents the sauce from curdling). Continue to pour in the oil and, if the sauce is too thick, add some more warm water. Aïoli can be served with potatoes but is usually one of the ingredients in Bourride (cf. recipe).

ed. Gisserot

LEMON JAM (Nice)

Preparation time: 3 days
Cooking time: approx. 2 hrs

- *1.5kg Nice lemons (approx 12 lemons)*
- *1.5kg sugar*
- *Water as required*

Wash 12 good quality lemons. Try to slice them thinly. Cover with water and leave to stand overnight. The next day, change the water and leave the slices to drip. Put the preserving pan on the heat and remove as soon as the liquid begins to boil. Leave to stand overnight. Drain the slices well, cover with cold water and simmer until the peel is soft (approx. 15 mins.) Make a syrup with ½ litre water and 1.5 kg caster sugar. Boil for 5 mins. then add the drained lemon slices. Simmer for a further 45 mins. (approximately). Check the consistency by setting a spoonful of jam to cool in the refrigerator. Fill sterilised jam jars up to the brim with the lemon jam.

This recipe was given to me by Mrs. Hélène Laurenti from Nice.

ORANGE WINE (Antibes)

Preparation time: 1 week
No cooking required

- 5 litres rosé (preferably good quality, not "plonk")
- 6 to 7 Seville oranges
- 1kg sugar
- 1 litre 90° proof alcohol
(sold in pharmacies in France)

Grate the orange zest. Mix with the wine, 90° proof alcohol and sugar in a preserving pan. Leave to stand for 1 week, stirring once or twice every day. Use a funnel and filter paper to filter the liquid into a bottle. Orange wine, which is now drunk as an aperitif, is one of the traditional specialities of Provence. Use it with peeled oranges to make quick jam by adding the same weight of sugar and simmering for 15 to 20 mins.

DESSERTS

Provençal cooking does not have many speciality desserts because the region supplies consumers with copious supplies of delicious fresh fruit. However, it would be a pity to ignore the culinary delights without which no festive meal would be complete. As to the thirteen desserts, they are an integral part of the Christmas meal. They consist of 4 "beggars" (almonds, hazelnuts, dried figs and walnuts), 4 fresh fruits (apples, pears, mandarins and winter melons are among the choices available), small biscuits, white and dark nougat and crystallised fruit, a speciality of the Nice and Apt regions. Added to that is the cake, the “pompe de Noël” or “gibassier”.

POMPE DE NOËL (Provençal Christmas Cake)

Preparation time: 30 mins. + 2 hrs. resting time for the dough
Cooking time: 20 mins.

- *1kg flour*
- *300g sugar*
- *¼ litre olive oil*
- *1 pinch salt*
- *20g baker's yeast*
- *2 dsp. orange flower water*

Put the flour on the working surface in a heap. Make a well in the middle and pour in the sugar, a pinch of salt, the olive oil and the baker's yeast (already diluted in warmed orange flower water). Knead well, adding a little water if required. Form a ball with the dough and place in a bowl. Cover with a cloth and leave in a temperate place for two hours. Roll out the dough to form ovals about 1cm (1/2 inch) thick. Using a knife, mark out a few elongated slits and place the ovals on an oiled baking sheet. Bake in a hot oven for 20 mins.

CHARD PIE
(known in Nice as "TOURTA DE BLEA")

Serves 16
Preparation time: 1½ hrs.
Cooking time: 35 mins.

Pastry:
- 550g flour
- 260g butter
- 100g caster sugar
- Water

Filling:
- 2 bunches Swiss chard
- 150g caster sugar
- 125g sultanas
- Pine nuts

Topping:
- 1 egg
- 5cl cold milk
- Icing sugar

Make a rich shortcrust pastry with all the ingredients indicated above. Set aside. Sort the chard – only the green leaves are used. Take care to remove all the large ribs then wash and dry the leaves. Divide the pastry into two unequal portions, setting aside the largest one for the top of the pie. Roll out the smaller portions and lay it on a large baking tray. Prick it with a fork then cover with the chard leaves. They can be cut with scissors or chopped but cutting gives a much better effect. Sweeten with 150g sugar then dot with sultanas and pine nuts. Spread the second portion of the pastry over the top and seal the edges. Brush with an egg beaten in some milk to produce a golden top then prick the top with a fork. Place in an oven set to Thermostat 6 or 7 for 20 mins. then turn down to 3 or 4 for the remainder of the baking time. As soon as the pie is removed from the oven, dredge with icing sugar to make it white. Once cooled, the pie should be cut into even pieces, either rectangles or squares.

GANSES (Carnival Doughnuts, Nice))

Makes a dozen doughnuts
Preparation time: 45 mins.
Cooking time: 10 mins.

- *1 sachet baking powder*
- *150gr caster sugar*
- *6 eggs*
- *500g flour*
- *1 glass rum (or 2 dsp. orange flower water)*
- *1 pinch salt*
- *Caster sugar*

photo Dufresse

Heap the flour on the working surface and break the eggs onto it. Then add the caster sugar, baking powder and pinch of salt. Moisten with water or rum and knead until the dough is smooth but fairly consistent. Form into a ball and leave to stand for 30 mins. covered with a cloth then rough portions of dough into small balls weighing approximately 50g each (the size of a small egg). Dust the surface with flour and roll out the balls of dough to give them an oval shape. They should be very thin. Using a knife, make three cross-cuts on each piece of dough, without allowing the cut to reach the edge of the oval. Place into a deep fat fryer and, when they are golden on both sides, drain them and lay on a serving dish. Dredge with icing sugar. "Ganses" are also known as "merveilles", "bugnes" or “oreillettes”. They keep for several days.

APPLE AND PINE NUT TART (Biot)

Serves 6
Preparation time: 30 mins.
Baking time: 35 mins.

- *250g flaky or shortcrust pastry (see recipe for shortcrust)*
- *5 or 6 apples*
  (or a combination of apples and pears depending on the season)
- *1 good handful of pine nuts*
- *4dsp. liquid honey (e.g. acacia)*
- *1 sachet vanilla sugar*
- *2tsp. cinnamon*
- *1dsp. orange flower water (optional)*
- *3 knobs butter*

photo Dufresse

Roll out the pastry and lay in a buttered pie tin. Prick the base with a fork. Roughly chop the apples and/or pears, add the pine nuts, orange flower water and vanilla sugar. Sprinkle with cinnamon and add 2 to 3 walnut sized knobs of butter on the fruit. Bake in a medium oven (approx. 200°) for 35 mins. When the tart is cooked and still hot, drizzle the liquid honey over the top. Serve warm or cold. Reduce the quality of honey slightly, to 3 dsp, if the tart seems to be very juicy otherwise the honey may run over the edges when it comes into contact with the hot tart.

MENTON-STYLE RICE (Menton)

Serves 5 - 6
Preparation time: 20 mins.
Cooking time: 10 mins.

- *150g white rice (preferably pudding rice)*
- *½ litre milk*
- *3 eggs (or 4 if they are small)*
- *5 dsp. caster sugar*
- *1 sachet vanilla sugar*
- *Zest of 1 grated lemon (optional)*
- *A few crystallised fruits and sultanas*
- *1 liqueur glass rum*
- *2 dsp. icing sugar*

ed. Gisserot

Wash the rice in cold water and cook in a little boiling water for 5 to 10 mins. until soft. Finely dice the crystallised fruit and macerate with the sultanas in the rum. Add the hot milk to the rice with the lemon zest. Add the sugar and vanilla sugar. Simmer over a low heat for 10 mins. Separate the eggs and beat the whites until stiff. Mix the yolks with a little cold milk and add to the rice mixture with the crystallised fruit, sultanas and half of the stiffly-beaten egg whites. Pour into a buttered ovenproof dish. Carefully spoon the remainder of the egg whites over the top and dredge with icing sugar. Place in a medium oven (Thermostat 5-6) until the egg whites are golden (approx. 10 mins.). Serve as soon as the dish has cooled.

VISITANDINE (Nice, Castagniers)

Serves 5 - 6
Preparation time: 15 mins.
Cooking time: 20 mins.

- *4 egg whites*
- *110g butter*
- *200g sugar*
- *100g flour*
- *1dsp. ground almonds*
- *½ packet baking powder*

Mix the sugar, melted butter, flour, ground almonds and baking powder. Beat the egg whites until stiff then gently fold into the cake mixture. Pour into a buttered sponge tin and bake in a medium oven (Thermostat 5 or 6) until the cake is slightly coloured but not golden.

photo Dufresse

SHORTCRUST PASTRY

Serves 5-6
Preparation time: 10 mins.
Cooking time: usually 25 mins. depending on the recipe

- *250g flour*
- *125g butter (slightly softened but not melted!)*
- *1 pinch salt*
- *Water*
- *1-2 dsp. sugar (for sweet shortcrust, used in desserts)*

Pour the flour into a mixing bowl and add the softened butter, cut into small cubes. Add a pinch of salt, and sugar if required. Mix the ingredients with your fingertips, adding a little water to obtain the correct consistency. The dough should be smooth and not too hard. It is not necessary to leave shortcrust to chill before using it.

FOUGASSETTES ("County" of Nice, Var hinterland)

Serves 5
Preparation time: 1 hr. in several stages
Standing time: 9 hours (6 + 3)
Cooking time: 20 mins.

- *1.1kg sieved flour*
- *Salted warm water*
- *50g oil*
- *10cl high-quality orange flower water*
- *1 very small pinch saffron*

Knead 100g sieved flour with ½ glass warm water to form a ball. Leave in a temperate place for six hours to ferment. Moisten the leaven with salted warm water and add it to 1kg of the same sieved flour. Also add 50g oil, 10cl very high-quality orange flower water (sold in pharmacies in France) and a very small pinch of saffron (the tip of a knife). Knead until the dough is smooth and leave to stand for a further three hours. Knead the dough again then roll it out to a thickness of two fingers. Make 5 or 6 fougassettes by rolling the dough into a figure-of-eight. Prick the surface and place the fougassettes on an oiled baking sheet. Place in the oven and bake at a very low temperature for 20 mins.

PINE NUT CROISSANTS (Provence) or "Pignolats"

Makes approx. 20 croissants
Preparation time: 30 mins.
Cooking time: 20 to 258 mins.

- *500g almonds or a sachet of ground almonds*
- *4 or 5 egg whites + 1 whole beaten egg*
- *A handful of pine nuts*
- *500g caster sugar*

Crush the almonds then use a pestle and mortar to grind them to a very fine powder (in this case, add a little caster sugar). Add the

photo Dufresse

500g sugar and mix into a fairly stiff dough, moistening with 4 or 5 egg whites. Form balls about the size of a walnut and roll them in the beaten egg. Roll the balls in the pine nuts, pulling them into shape you go. The pine nuts should stick to the dough. Then curve the dough slightly to form a croissant shape and bake on a buttered baking tray in a moderate oven.

WINES OF PROVENCE

Provence is a land of sunshine and it produces excellent, full-bodied wines. The main grape variety used is Mourvedre but Grenache and Cinsaut are not uncommon. The rosés are famous but the region also produces some high-quality reds and whites.

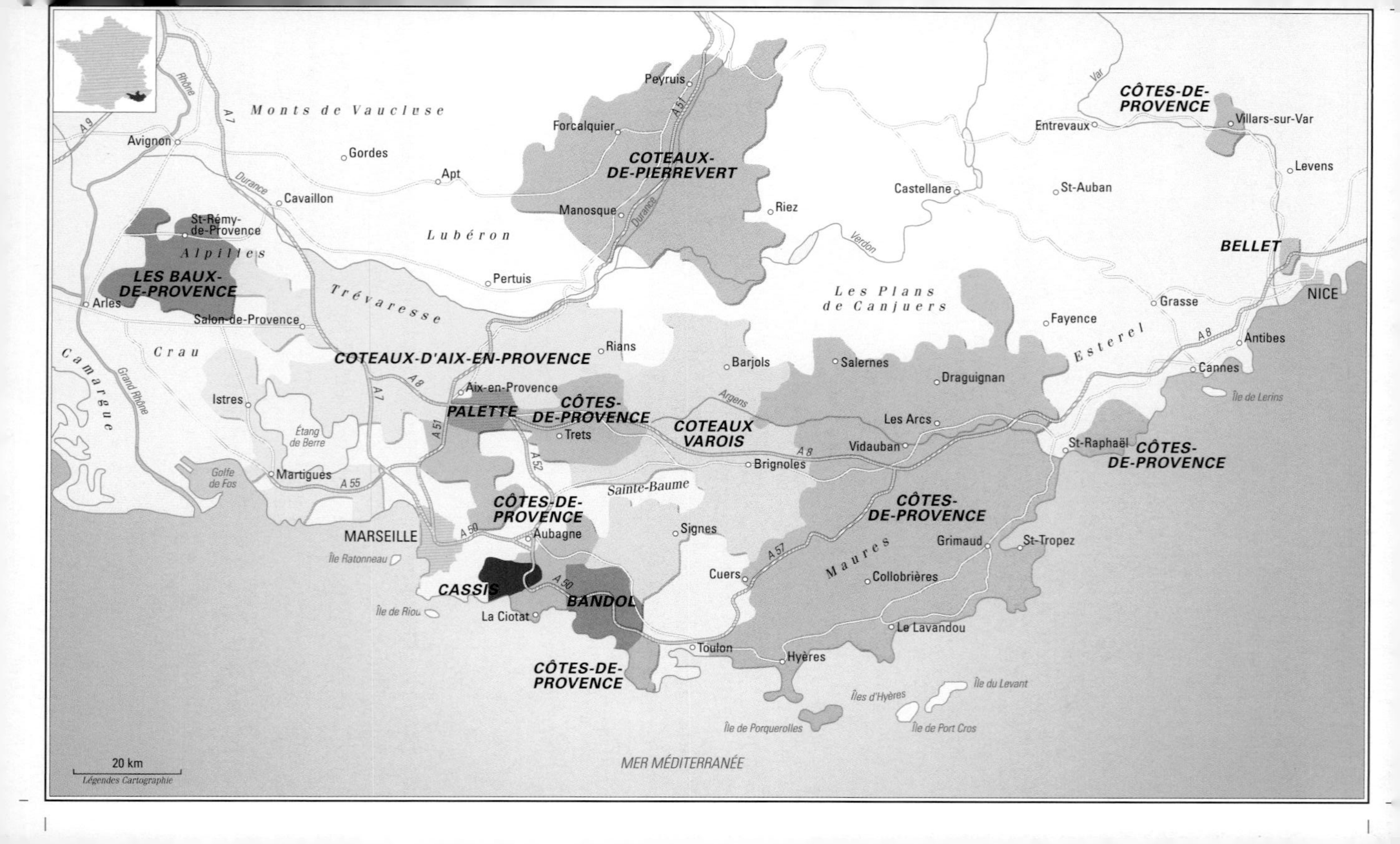
Monts de Vaucluse
Avignon
Rhône
A9
A7
Gordes
Apt
Durance
Cavaillon
St-Rémy-de-Provence
Alpilles
Lubéron
LES BAUX-DE-PROVENCE
Arles
Pertuis
Trévaresse
Salon-de-Provence
Crau
Camargue
Grand Rhône
COTEAUX-D'AIX-EN-PROVENCE
Rians
Istres
Aix-en-Provence
A8
PALETTE
CÔTES-DE-PROVENCE
Trets
A51
Étang de Berre
Golfe de Fos
Martigues
A 55
A 52
CÔTES-DE-PROVENCE
MARSEILLE
A 50
Aubagne
Île Ratonneau
CASSIS
Île de Riou
La Ciotat
A 50
BANDOL
CÔTES-DE-PROVENCE
Peyruis
Forcalquier
A 51
COTEAUX-DE-PIERREVERT
Manosque
Riez
Barjols
COTEAUX VAROIS
Brignoles
Sainte-Baume
Signes
Cuers
Toulon
A 57
Hyères
Île de Porquerolles
Îles d'Hyères
Île de Port Cros
Île du Levant
Les Plans de Canjuers
Verdon
Castellane
Salernes
Draguignan
Argens
Les Arcs
Vidauban
A 8
CÔTES-DE-PROVENCE
Maures
Collobrières
Grimaud
St-Tropez
Le Lavandou
St-Raphaël
CÔTES-DE-PROVENCE
Esterel
Fayence
Grasse
A8
Antibes
Cannes
Île de Lerins
NICE
BELLET
Entrevaux
Var
CÔTES-DE-PROVENCE
Villars-sur-Var
Levens
St-Auban
MER MÉDITERRANÉE
20 km
Légendes Cartographie

CHEESES OF PROVENCE

Provence is a region of goats but it also produces some wonderful ewe’s milk specialities.

The best known of the Provençal cheeses is Banon made from goat’s milk and occasionally from ewe's and cow's milk.

Other wonderful cheeses include Annot, Tomme de Sospel, Picodon de Valréas, Tomme du Ventoux, Tomme de Camargue, Tomme de Valberg and Brousse de la Vésubie or Brousse du Rove.

ed. Gisserot

TABLE OF CONTENTS

FISH

MEAT

PASTA

VEGETABLES AND GARNISHES

PRESERVES & SPECIALITIES

DESSERTS

TOULON

Photo Captions

Page 1 : Poppies

Page 2 : A fountain in the mediaeval village of Vaison.

Page 4 : Alphone Daudet's windmill in Fontvieille.

Pages 6-7 : A panoramic view from Pourrières over the Sainte-Victoire mountain range.

Pages 28-29 : A view eastwards from Les Baux, set on its clifftop.

Page 49 (top) : The most famous aqueduct in the world, the Pont du Gard.

Page 49 (bottom) : The Verdon Gorge.

Page 50 (top) : Sheep grazing on Mont Ventoux.

Page 50 (bottom) : A "ranch" in Camargue.

Pages 64-65 : The harbour in Saint-Tropez.

Pages 76-77 : The citadel in Sisteron reflected in the waters of the River Durance.

Page 78 : The bell tower in Saint-Tropez.

Page 96 : Moustiers-Sainte-Marie in its superb mountain setting, famous all over the world for its outstanding delftware.

Page 116 : Countryside around Les Baux.

Page 119 : The village of Méthanis.

Page 121 : A horse in Camargue.

Page 122 (top) : A close-up of the Four Dolphins Fountain in Aix-en-Provence.

Page 122 (bottom) : Fontaine-de-Vaucluse, where the rivers flows past lush, green banks.

Page 127 : The old tower on the town walls in Saint-Tropez.

Imprimé par Pollina 85 Luçon n° d'impression : L45988
Imprimé en France